SERIOUSLY TRUE MYSTERIES

THE CASE OF THE

Missing Arctic Fox

and Other True Animal Mysteries for You to Solve

by Heather L. Montgomery

Consultant: Dwight Lawson, PhD
Deputy Director | Zoo Atlanta

CAPSTONE PRESS
a capstone imprint

Fact Finders are published by Capstone Press,
1710 Roe Crest Drive, North Mankato, Minnesota 56003.
www.capstonepub.com

 Books published by Capstone Press are manufactured with paper
containing at least 10 percent post-consumer waste.

Library of Congress Cataloging-in-Publication Data
Montgomery, Heather L.
The case of the missing arctic fox and other true animal mysteries for you to solve / by Heather L. Montgomery.
p. cm.—(Fact finders. Seriously true mysteries.)
Includes bibliographical references and index.
Summary: "Nonfiction animal information is presented as mysteries for readers to solve. With the turn of a page, readers
learn how to solve the true animal mystery"—Provided by publisher.
ISBN 978-1-4296-7625-0 (library binding)
1. Animals—Miscellanea—Juvenile literature. I. Title. II. Series.
QL49.M7923 2012
590—dc23   2011026684

Editorial Credits
Jennifer Besel, editor; Tracy Davies McCabe, designer; Wanda Winch, media researcher;
    Laura Manthe, production specialist

Photo Credits
Alamy: John Cancalosi, 26 (bottom); Dreamstime: Derrick Neil, 24 (bottom), Outdoorsman, 6 (owl); Getty Images Inc: Stone/Tim Flach, 24
(top); iStockphoto: DNY59, 17 (br), 18 (br), 23 (newspaper), Nicholas Belton, 7 (br), Savushkin, 4 (fur), 9 (back), 10 (back), 29 (fur); Newscom:
Danita Delimont/Paul Souders, 23 (paw print); SeaPics.com: David Wrobel, 16 (bl); Shutterstock: alarifoto, cover (owl), Allesandro Vigano,
cover (fox), Andrea Danti, 18 (bl), Andreas Algenburger, 19 (back), 20 (back), Anna Segeren, cover (water), Apostrophe, 9 (middle), Becky
Sheridan, 10 (bl), Chantal de bruijne, 13 (bottom), Charlie Edward, 5, (bottom), 6 (bottom), Dgrilla, cover (sign), Dr. Morley Read, 6 (pellet),
Eky Studio, 21 (back), 22 (back), Elena Elisseeva, cover (tree), Eric Isselée, 11 (br), 12 (bl, br), Falk Kienas, cover (paw print), fivespots, cover
(snake), 8 (snake), Imagix, 20 (top), Irina Tischenko, 28 (middle), Jason Patrick Ross, cover (cave), Kayros Studio "Be Happy!", 15 (middle),
khz, 9 (bottom), kirsanov, cover (bat), 18 (bat), Kruglov_Orda, 17 (bat), L_amica, 16 (back), Larry B. King, 25 (bottom), Lonnie Gorsline, 25
(back), 26 (back), Map Resources, 17 (back), 18 (back), masonjar, 7 (forest), 8 (forest), Michael Pettigrew, 22 (br), Michelangelus, 27 (back),
28 (back), Natursports, 14 (bottom), Olena Chyrko, 21 (middle), 22 (middle), Oriontrail, 5 (back), 6 (back), pandapaw, 12 (bm), prudkov, 15
(back), re_bekka, 11 (map), 12 (map), R-studio, 24 (paper), Sam DCruz, 11 (back), 12 (back), Sergey Galushko, 4 (prints), 29 (left), Slasha, 13
(back), 14(back), Studio DMM Photography, Designs & Art, 5 (middle), 6 (middle), Svetlana Ivanova, 11 (art design), 12 (art design), Triff,
23 (back), 24 (back), visceralimage, 20 (bottom), Vlue, 7 (top), 8 (top); www.AfricanHuntingSafaris.com, Ozondjahe Safaris, 12 (middle);
www.marinethemes.com: Kelvin Aitken, 16 (br)

Printed in the United States of America in Brainerd, Minnesota.
102011   006406BANGS12

TABLE OF CONTENTS

TRACKING DOWN
ANSWERS

Squirrels chewing snake skins? Footprints mysteriously made in the night? Vanishing animals? Animal mysteries lurk all around you. They prowl the forests and fields, waiting to be solved. Grab your magnifying glass. You have some animal mysteries to solve.

To put these mysteries to rest, you'll need all your detective skills. Don't miss a tiny fossil, ignore a bone, or forget to explore the surroundings. Put the clues together to solve the mysteries.

BEFORE CONTINUING, PLEASE STATE THE ANIMAL DETECTIVE'S PROMISE:

I will read each one-page mystery completely. I will try to solve each mystery to the best of my ability. I will not use this book as scratch paper. I will not peek at the answer on the flip side of the page. Only after I have solved the mystery or worn down my brain trying may I turn the page.

Now you're ready for some toad-ally tricky animal mysteries. What are you waiting for? Get mooooving!

SNOW ANGELS?

January 4
6:00 a.m.
28° F (-2° C), no wind
St. Mary's, PA
pasture, southwest of barn

Found tiny tracks running across the snowy pasture. Each track was just ¼ inch (.6 centimeter) long. Followed the tracks for 6 feet (2 meters) into the wide-open pasture. Suddenly, the tracks disappeared. At the trail's end, there were two crescent-shaped marks that looked like a small snow angel. Under a maple tree nearby, discovered bones and fur packed together in a tight gray ball.

What happened here last night?

A MIDNIGHT SNACK

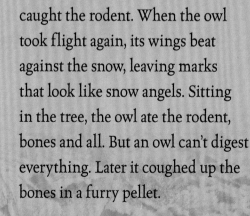

Scientists can't always find the actual animals when there's a mystery to solve. But often they can find clues like animal tracks. These clues help show how animals act in nature.

The tracks in the snow in this mystery have four toes on the front foot and five toes on the hind foot. **Rodent** tracks usually look like that. Many rodents are small and live in pastures. It's likely the small tracks belong to some kind of rodent.

The crescent-shaped marks at the end of the tracks are the shape of an owl's outstretched wing. Birds eat rodents. So …

From the clues we can re-create what happened. A hungry owl spotted a rodent in the moonlight. It swooped down and caught the rodent. When the owl took flight again, its wings beat against the snow, leaving marks that look like snow angels. Sitting in the tree, the owl ate the rodent, bones and all. But an owl can't digest everything. Later it coughed up the bones in a furry pellet.

an owl pellet

rodent—a mammal with long front teeth used for gnawing

6

HEADS OR TAILS?

Hiking through a swamp in southeastern Asia, you discover a snake skin. The skin is 28 feet (8.5 m) long! The head of the skin is caught on a dead log to your right, and the tail stretches out to the left. You wonder what kind of snake it's from. It could be dangerous. You'd rather not run into a huge snake in the middle of a swamp.

WHICH WAY SHOULD YOU GO?

INSIDE OUT

In the swamps of Asia, any snake that long would have to be a python. Although a python could kill a human, its normal prey is birds and small animals. But you still wouldn't want to step on this snake. So which way should you go to avoid it?

To figure that out, think about how a snake sheds its skin. When it gets too large for its skin, the snake rubs against a log to split the skin near its mouth. The skin from the snake's head sticks to the log. As the snake sheds, the skin peels backward, turning inside out like a sock.

The last part of the snake to pull out of the skin was the tail. So the tail of the shed skin points in the direction the snake slithered. To avoid the snake, go the way the head points.

a Burmese python

Globe-Trotter

Hi Zoe!

My vacation here in America is going well! I just accidentally scared a wild animal. It was fuzzy and gray and climbing out of a tree. When I surprised it, it rolled over and played dead! Believe it or not, it is a cousin to the kangaroos we have back home.

Good day, mate!

Maddie

What animal did Maddie surprise?

Maddie Walker
107 Park Headquarters Road
Gatlinburg, TN 37738
United States of America

Zoe Nguyen
Ruby Road
Charter's Towers, QLD 4820
Australia

9

Migrating Marsupials

What animal plays dead and is related to kangaroos? The animal is an opossum! The opossum is a North American **marsupial**. Although they don't look alike, opossums and kangaroos are cousins. Both have a pouch used for carrying their babies.

How can animals living across the ocean from each other be related? They come from a common **ancestor**. More than 125 million years ago, Earth's continents were connected. An early type of marsupial lived in what is now Asia. Over time the plates in Earth's crust moved the land, shifting and breaking apart the continents. As the continents broke apart, the marsupials were divided and scattered around the world. Over time the animals changed to survive in their new environments. But they all kept their pouches.

a baby opossum

marsupial—an animal that carries its young in a pouch
ancestor—a member of a family that lived a long time ago

BATTLEGROUND

In the grasslands of Africa, there are signs of a battle. The ground has been churned up by hundreds of hooves. The hoof prints show two separate toes that make a pear-shaped print. Parts from an animal are scattered across the ground. Based on the size of the parts, the animal was almost 5 feet (1.5 m) tall. A jawbone left in the dust has bladelike teeth in the front and flat, wide teeth in the back. In the distance a lion returns to its pride.

WHAT ANIMAL LOST THIS BATTLE?

The prints found all around look like these.

THE TEETH TELL THE TALE

The jawbone is the key to unlocking this mystery. It has bladelike front teeth. Those teeth would be good for chopping grass. It also has flat back teeth, perfect for grinding plants. The dead animal must have been a **herbivore**.

The hoof prints hint that a large herd of creatures was running through the area. Herbivores often travel in herds for protection. Many herbivores have hooves. Putting the clues together, you can determine that a **predator** attacked a herd of herbivores and killed one for food.

wildebeest hoof

But what herbivore was it? In the African grassland, zebras, wildebeests, and even hippopotamuses travel in herds. Here's where the tracks can help narrow it down. The track of a zebra's single toe is shaped like a horseshoe. So it couldn't have been a zebra. Hippo tracks have four big toes. The prints and jaw match those of a wildebeest.

A herd of wildebeest must have been attacked. A predator, such as a lion, caught one for food.

zebra

wildebeest

hippo

herbivore—an animal that eats only plants
predator—an animal that hunts other animals for food

Something's Fishy!

Walking through a dark, damp cave in northern Alabama, you come to a sign.

"The limestone walls of this cave were formed more than 500 million years ago. During that time only simple creatures without backbones existed."

In the next room, a tour guide points to a fossil in the rock. The bumps in the fossil are in a line. Things that look like tiny ribs stick out on each side of the line. A man in the group says, "A fish skeleton! Imagine ancient fish swimming right past you."

The tour guide says, "I'm afraid that couldn't have happened."

Why not?

Back Before Bones

The clues to solve this mystery are in the sign. Did you catch them? The sign says that when the limestone walls were formed, there were only animals without backbones.

Fish have backbones, so they couldn't have been there when the walls were forming. The fossil in the rock is actually of an **invertebrate**. The creature's body was made of many segments. The segments may look like a backbone. But really these segments were on the outside of the animal's body. It was not until millions of years later that fish and other animals with backbones developed from invertebrates.

a fossil of an invertebrate called a trilobite

How did the ancient invertebrate get into the rock? An ocean once covered the place where the cave now stands. As invertebrates in the ocean died, they sank to the bottom. Their skeletons piled up, pressed together, and formed the rock called limestone. Later, water tunneled through that limestone, creating the cave.

invertebrate—an animal without a backbone

From the Field

To: you@trueanimalmysteries.com
Cc:

Subject: Found Pig and Coffin!

Hello!

I'm having a great time on this research expedition. Jason just came up from a mission. We discovered a pig and a coffin. We shot a great photo of the coffin while it was fishing!

I'm so glad we have Jason to do the hard work. It must be so cold and dark down there. With all the pressure, I know I would be crushed!

Take care, and see you in about a month.

Dr. García

What are Dr. García and Jason exploring?

Into the Deep

The mystery place is cold, dark, and has enough pressure to crush a person. But it's home to a pig and a coffin that fishes. Where is this place?

This place is the bottom of the ocean. Water is heavy. As a person or animal dives down into water, the amount of water above them increases. That water pushes on the body, creating extreme pressure. The water pressure at the bottom of the ocean is strong enough to crush a human's body.

But many animals have **adapted** to that cold, dark, heavy world. The pig in the mystery is a sea pig. It can live as far down as 6.2 miles (10 kilometers)!

Deep-sea creatures also have to deal with an environment with little food. The sea pig solves that problem by slurping up dead animals that fall to the sea floor. The fishing coffin is really the coffinfish. This animal dangles a small piece of flesh above its head. The bait lures in small animals for supper.

Scientists who study the deepest parts of the ocean need tools to help them. Jason isn't a person. It's actually a remotely operated vehicle (ROV). From boats, scientists send ROVs down into the deep sea. ROVs take pictures and collect animal samples. They can also collect water, soil samples, and temperature information.

Sea pigs eat mud on the sea floor.

The coffinfish's dangling lure often hides in its snout.

adapt—to change in order to survive

NORTH OR SOUTH?

A group of scientists did an experiment on bats in 2007. Over the course of a month, the scientists caught 30 bats. Each night they exposed a few bats to a strong magnet. The scientists then took the bats miles north of their home, and let them go. Most of the bats reacted the same way. They tried to fly back home, but they flew farther north instead of south.

WHY DID THE BATS FLY THE WRONG WAY?

COMPASS CONFUSION

People use compasses to find their way. A compass has a small metal magnet called a needle. The Earth is also a magnet. A **magnetic field** surrounds the entire planet. The Earth's magnetic field and a compass' needle attract each other. The needle spins to point toward Earth's magnetic north. But Earth's magnetic field is fairly weak. Put another magnet near the compass, and the needle will be attracted to the nearby magnet instead.

Bats, birds, and some other animals have bits of metal in their bodies. These metal pieces act like compasses, helping the animals find their way home after long flights.

When researchers put the bats near the strong magnet, their internal compasses changed. Their metal pieces were attracted to the magnet, not Earth's magnetic field. So the bats thought north was south.

On a side note, the bats did find their way home after a few hours. Their compass may have realigned or they used their other senses to figure it out. Scientists are still studying that part!

This illustration shows Earth's magnetic field. The metal in bats is attracted to the magnetic poles shown in blue shading at the top and bottom.

magnetic field—the space near a magnetic body or current-carrying body in which magnetic forces can be detected

TOTAL TRICKSTER

In early January, a wildlife magazine hires you to take pictures of an arctic fox. On your way to the airport, you realize you don't know what an arctic fox looks like. Just before your flight, you do some quick research. You read on the Internet that it's a gray-brown fox that's about 20 inches (51 cm) long.

At the arctic outpost, someone points out where a fox has been seen hunting every night. Getting the shots you need should be easy. You crunch your way across the snow to set up your camera. You wait. A white shape moves across the snow, but you ignore it. You are looking for a fox with dark fur. Your feet freeze as you wait all night. But you never see a fox. The same thing happens the next night.

On the third day, a scientist says he saw the fox both nights.

WHY DIDN'T YOU?

WINTER WHITE

Animals have adaptations to keep them alive. Deep-sea animals have bodies that can handle enormous water pressure. Other animals use **camouflage** to stay hidden from predators. Some animals are always camouflaged. Certain species of butterflies and katydids look just like dead leaves. Other animals change color as their surroundings change. The information that said the fox had a gray-brown coat was only half correct. Arctic foxes use camouflage too.

The fox was nearby, but it had changed color. The white shape moving across the snow was an arctic fox. During summer arctic foxes do have a gray-brown coat. This color blends in with the foxes' surroundings. But in winter, arctic foxes turn white. Their fur matches the snow and ice that covers the arctic ground.

Weasels, caribou, and arctic hares use this kind of camouflage too. Some animals, such as arctic foxes and hares, turn completely white. Others, such as caribou, only turn partially white. Each type of animal adapts to its specific area.

camouflage—coloring or covering that makes animals look like their surroundings

MOST WANTED

A group of criminals is wanted
for the following offenses:

1. Trespassing
Suspects were seen on and in people's
homes and walking into their mouths
without permission.

2. Polluting
Suspects release a nasty liquid that
stinks up the air.

3. Robbery
Suspects also steal food from locals.

Suspects are often considered female
because of their name. But the group has
both male and female members.

Who are these sneaky, smelly thieves?

Bad Bugs

These stinky, stealing trespassers are a problem for a lot of people. Who are they?

These bad guys are bugs! Specifically, they are ladybugs called Asian lady beetles. People brought the beetle from Asia to North America to eat pests off crops. The Asian lady beetles did a good job of that. But then they spread away from crops into homes and schools. They have become an **invasive species**.

In the fall these beetles look for a place to spend the winter. They crawl on houses, trying to find a way in. Eager to find a warm spot, they sometimes climb on people and into their mouths. When spring returns the beetles emerge. They are hungry, and they steal and eat the food of local ladybugs.

When scared, the lady beetles become polluters too. They drip yellow liquid from their leg joints. In nature that liquid works to scare away predators. In houses it stains walls and makes a big stink.

Today these beetle invaders have spread throughout North America and around the world. Scientists are tracking these bugs to find ways to keep them from damaging local **ecosystems.**

Asian lady beetle

invasive species—a plant or animal that has spread into a new ecosystem
ecosystem—a group of animals, plants, and nonliving things that interact in an area

BIGFOOT!

August 3

NEWSY TIMES

BIGFOOT IN THE PARK?

Reports emerged today of a Bigfoot that may have wandered through Yellowstone National Park. A park visitor spotted a large animal crossing a parking lot. Researchers who follow Bigfoots believe the mysterious animals are apelike creatures. Some reports put the

Some believe these tracks are from a Bigfoot.

creatures at 9 feet (2.7 m) tall and 1,000 pounds (454 kilograms).

"It was huge," said the park visitor. "It had to be Bigfoot. I got a picture of its footprints. They were more than 9 inches long! That's 23 centimeters for you scientists."

August 4

NEWSY TIMES

SCIENTISTS CONFIRM BIGFOOT SIGHTING WAS A FAKE.

HOW DID THE SCIENTISTS KNOW THERE WASN'T A BIGFOOT SIGHTING?

BELIEVE IT OR NOT

The key to unlocking this mystery is in the tracks. When people find tracks that might belong to a Bigfoot, researchers compare them to those of known animals. They consider where the tracks were found and their shape and size. The tracks in the newspaper were about 9 inches (23 cm) long. They show that the strongest toe is on the outside of the creature's foot. Claw marks can also be seen in the tracks.

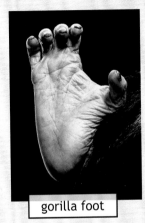

gorilla foot

Compare the tracks to an ape's foot. If it is apelike, a Bigfoot's biggest toe should be on the inside of its foot. That's not what's seen in the tracks.

The 9-inch (23-cm) tracks are also smaller than an average gorilla's tracks. Gorillas have feet around 12 inches (30 cm) long. Apes don't have claws, either.

The footprints are not similar enough to an ape's foot to be from any apelike creature. But they are from an animal that is known to live in Yellowstone. The tracks are from a grizzly bear. The bears have claws. They also have a 5- to 10-inch (13- to 25-cm) footprint. The tracks in the paper are just the right size for a grizzly bear.

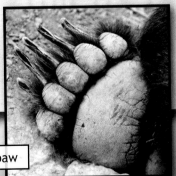

grizzly bear paw

Chew On This!

A California ground squirrel scampers through a park. It searches for food and keeps an eye out for snakes. It avoids snakes but not snake skins. When it discovers a shed rattlesnake skin, it shoves the skin in its mouth. It begins to chew. Then the squirrel licks its fur. The squirrel smears the snake-flavored spit all over its sides, tail, and even its rear end!

Why would a squirrel do something so gross?

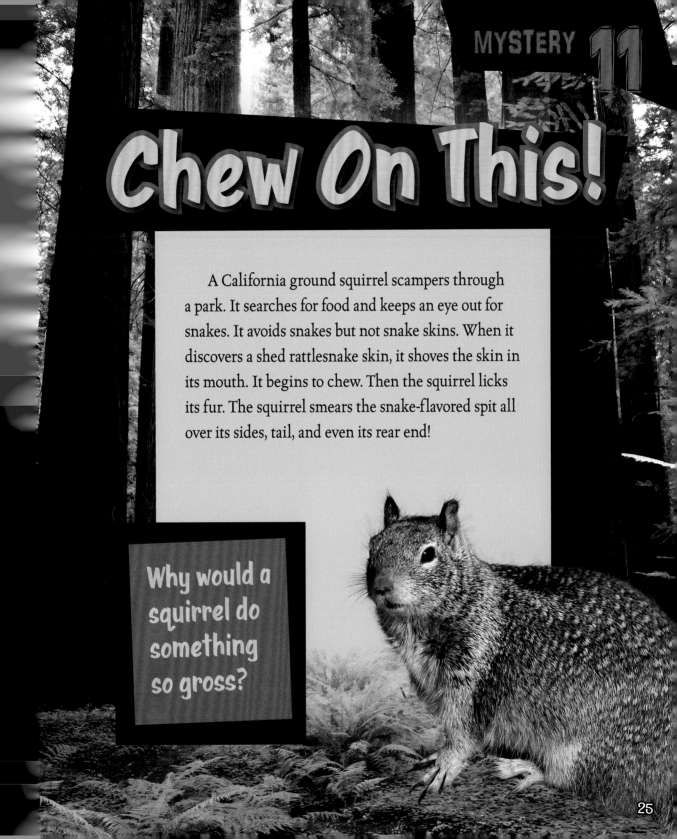

Smelly Spit

Rattlesnakes prey on squirrels. To find their next meal, snakes rely on their sense of smell. They flick out their tongues to smell the air for squirrels or other tasty foods. But when the squirrel is covered in snake-flavored spit, what do you think snakes smell?

The California ground squirrels have developed smelly camouflage to hide from the snakes. After chewing rattlesnake skin, a squirrel's spit is full of bits of snake skin. When the squirrel licks itself, the spit carries the snake skin onto the squirrel's fur. The odor of the rattlesnake skin masks the odor of the squirrel. The squirrel is camouflaged by smell!

BLOOD-FILLED BEAST

This creature:

- has trillions of bacteria squirming in its guts.
- is full of blood; lined up, its blood vessels could wrap around the world twice.
- makes pee that is clean enough to drink.
- begins life with 94 more bones than it has when it dies.
- contains a brain that weighs 3 pounds (1.4 kg).
- can survive only a few minutes without air.

WHAT ANIMAL IS IT?

LOOK INSIDE

The answer to this mystery is very close. The animal is YOU!

Just like other animals, your body is full of amazing systems that keep you alive. The bacteria in your stomach tear down food so you can digest it. Without bacteria in there, you would starve. The digested food whips through miles of blood vessels to feed your lungs, muscles, and organs.

One organ, the kidney, cleans the blood and creates pee. Although the urine is **sterile**, it is full of waste. You wouldn't want to drink it!

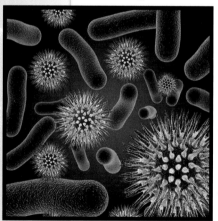

Your blood was made in your bones. Bones also give your body structure. When you were born, many of your bones were soft. As you age, some of the bones grow together and harden into single bones. Adults have fewer bones than children.

Blood also carries the all-important gas—oxygen. Your brain, the control tower of your body, needs oxygen to survive. Without it, you'd be dead.

sterile—free of germs

THAT'S A WRAP!

HERE'S ONE LAST MYSTERY. WHAT DO THE CLUES DESCRIBE?

Some walk on two legs
Others move on four.
Still others use their wings to fly
Or their fins to soar.

They are found most anywhere—
In dirt, and sky, and sea.
There are many members in their group.
In fact, one member's ME!

The clues describe animals! Mysteries of the animal world surround you. Solving them helps you understand how humans and our animal neighbors affect the planet. So get going! Animal mysteries are waiting to be solved …

GLOSSARY

adapt (uh-DAPT)—to change in order to survive; a change in an animal or plant is called an adaptation

ancestor (AN-ses-tuhr)—a member of a family that lived a long time ago

camouflage (KA-muh-flahzh)—coloring or covering that makes animals, people, and objects look like their surroundings

ecosystem (EE-koh-sis-tuhm)—a group of animals, plants, and nonliving things that interact in an area

herbivore (HUR-buh-vor)—an animal that eats only plants

invasive species (in-VEY-siv SPEE-sheez)—a plant or animal that has spread into a new ecosystem

invertebrate (in-VUR-tuh-bruht)—an animal without a backbone

magnetic field (mag-NE-tik FEELD)—the space near a magnetic body or current-carrying body in which magnetic forces can be detected

marsupial (mar-SOO-pee-uhl)—a group of mammals in which the females feed and carry their young in pouches

predator (PRED-uh-tur)—an animal that hunts other animals for food

rodent (ROHD-uhnt)—a mammal with long front teeth used for gnawing; rats, mice, and squirrels are rodents

sterile (STER-uhl)—free of germs

READ MORE

Bow, James. *Animal Mysteries Revealed*. Mysteries Revealed. New York: Crabtree Pub., 2010.

Gilpin, Daniel. *Record-Breaking Animals*. Record Breakers. New York: PowerKids Press, 2012.

Stille, Darlene R. *The Case of the Soda Explosion and Other True Science Mysteries for You to Solve*. Seriously True Mysteries. Mankato, Minn.: Capstone Press, 2012.

INTERNET SITES

FactHound offers a safe, fun way to find Internet sites related to this book. All of the sites on FactHound have been researched by our staff.

Here's all you do:

Visit www.facthound.com

Type in this code: 9781429676250

Check out projects, games and lots more at
www.capstonekids.com

INDEX